Plain Verses

Caroline Cynthia

BookLeaf
Publishing

India | USA | UK

Presentation by *BookLeaf Publishing*

Web: www.bookleafpub.com

E-mail: info@bookleafpub.com

ISBN: 9789357448956

First edition 2022

For my Church, Philadelphia fellowship
Villivakkam for helping me learn, observe, and
grow with you as a disciple of Christ Jesus.

ACKNOWLEDGEMENT

I wish to express my gratitude to my sister, Annie, for setting me up and pushing me to write this. Grateful to Bookleaf publishing, who gave me firm deadlines which compelled me to finish what I started. My parents, Prema and Prabakaran who bought me so many books and kindled in me the love for reading and writing, gave me the freedom to think and the space to create.

Thankful to my husband and best friend, Jesudawson Charles, for his incredible heart and invaluable support in everything I want to do. My children, Arpana and Seeshan, for inspiring me every day to be a person worthy of them.

I am indebted to those who read my occasional posts and scribbles. You encourage me with your great comments. I read and savour every one of them. Thank you for listening to my stories. Thank you for using your gift of encouragement to help an amateur.

I'm thankful to God for the resources that He's placed in my life. Without Christ, there's nothing in my life worth writing about.

PREFACE

Writing for me is therapeutic. I write for myself to make myself accountable. Sometimes, I share my stories for others to read. The verses in these poems do not have powerful metaphors or solid poetic devices. They are plain verses prompted by different feelings.

It is one thing to be inspired by out of the world experiences. But it is a gift to learn from the mundane monotony of life. My verses seek to embrace the ordinary and cherish it. Because if we miss the simple moments of life, we are at a loss indeed.

"Write the vision...make it plain." - Habakkuk 2:2 (The Bible)

We Don't Want to Bury No More

Of the many works you gave us, Lord.
One was to bury the dead.
To say goodbye in a fitting way
And thank You for the life they led.

At every funeral service, Lord
We preached hope in death and life in Christ.
Though we miss every bit of the person we bury,
We know that he hasn't ceased to exist
But just in a place that we can't go to yet.

But now, Lord
I'm asking You,
I don't want to bury
Don't let my people go
To a place where I cannot see their beautiful
lives anymore.

I need Your people, more than You do, Lord.
Each soul is a miracle in time
Because of Your love that binds us deep
It feels like they are mine.

Yes, God, so much we need You
But Oh, how much we need each other too.

Forgive me, Lord
Don't take away because we didn't care
Give me a chance just one more time.
And we promise to be more loving and kind.

You do not live in houses made by human hands,
You only live in bodies that Your hands have
made.
Every time you let someone fade,
It feels like a part of You
Has gone away too.

I know that I am not a saint.
Just another sinner,
Who has lost my way in grief and sorrow,
Because I don't want to bury another body
tomorrow.

Amen.

Faithful Servant

Don't give me another option
Lord, I don't want many open doors
My life is Your breath in action
And it is Your will that I adore

When I look inside to feel
The deep desires in me
Roaring emotions slowly fade
And only the gentle sound of Your heartbeat
remains.

Trying to focus,
And struggling to find.
The reason for my life.
Lord, what were your thoughts for me?
When I was nowhere else but in Your mind?

Your perfect life
Teaches me how to live and walk
Your selfless death
Makes me wonder
Why did you care about me so much at all?
Your resurrection my King
Proves your power and dominion
Above all that I behold in awe.

Life goes on here for a few years alone.
The rest I spend in an eternity
Irresistible, though unknown

With arms open wide
Master, you are waiting for me.
To show me my mansion
And Your glory to reveal

When you hold me in your arms
I want you to say
"Well done faithful servant
You've always known my heart
And obeyed my voice
Even through troubled paths"

In this life Father
My strength will always fail.
Oh Lord, My Master
Let your Grace alone prevail.

The Caregiver

The destination never arrives
Most days, hard decisions come by
An immense burden to carry
Caring for the sick
Makes you weak and weary

Though we see their pain and suffering
Sometimes we lack in understanding
The frazzled mind cannot absorb
Their hurtful actions
In hopelessness and frustration

When so much has been done
And you are on this path alone
Most days, time is never your own
Sometimes you feel, you cannot go on.

Ask for daily bread
Grace for each day
The Lord is near to those who call
Even if it feels like He is not there at all

He is the Rock Eternal
He knows your endless sobbing
He knows you want to withdraw sometimes
But He gently prods you every time

To be strong
To keep at it

He will give the words to speak
The strength to serve
And the love to reflect Him
In all you do each day

At the end
You will be in perfect peace
Because of all the love you showed
Showers of mercy heaven will bestow.

A Writer's Prayer

When I want to write,
I take my Bible to the light
The wondrous things You've written
I pray that I must see
The encouragement, the correction
And the message spelt out for me.

My inner life
Is a strange mix
Of Your motivations and mine,
Please let me express
Only what's in Your mind.

Every moment of my life, I want to stay within
Your will
But sometimes, in my hastiness
I can't surrender and stay still.

Woven in every season
Of this weary life of mine,
Please help me find a story,
Where ordinary meets the Divine
To bring healing to those in pain
And bring Hope to those who complain.

Let me not compete

Because my competence comes from You.
You are the True Vine
In You, my words bear fruit.

Sometimes, when I'm exhausted
And though I see no gain,
Lord, please help me persevere,
Don't let my labor go in vain.

Lord, teach me to be concise
Let my readers hear,
I want to talk to them,
With a voice,
That they hold dear.

There will come a day,
When the thoughts won't come,
And my words go numb,
Stay beside me,
And let me know

That I have been faithful and my race is done.

Proverbs 32 - A Husband of Noble Character

An excellent husband, no one can find
To his value, all money resigns.
He's forever calm;
In her love, that remains.
He trusts in his wife
Beyond all other gains.

When she gets angry
And she's fuming out stress
Her crazy moods
He doesn't mind
So strong is his love
That is patient and kind.

He does not complain
about her choices.
And he doesn't take for granted
Her generous sacrifices
He values her life,
More than the money she brings
His favourite music
Is the song she sings.

He is her best critic
The anchor for her dreams

He's proud of her achievements
He knows that she's unique.

The beauty he sees,
Is the beauty that never fades.
It's her heart that charms him
Today and always,

As her waistline broadens
Her body loses grace.
Years begin to creep in
And draw indelible lines on her face

But he loves her even more,
This wife of his youth.
Each day, he learns her better.
And remains to her, forever true

Husbands can't be everything you need.
Poor guys! They don't have a clue
Because
There is no Proverbs thirty-two

Wait to Understand

When the seas are raging
Thunderstorms demoralize
I'm in your boat
And by your side.

I only need a word to command the winds you
see;
But I don't do it so fast
Because;
Then you'll take your eyes off of me.

In the midst of the tempest
I love it when you cling to My arm
With lots of fear inside
Yet a tinge of faith that's still
And holding on.

I see beyond that plastic smile
Deeper than the reasons on your tongue
Your thoughts, before they were born
And the life for which you long

Your pain before it even hurts you
Unsaid prayers in the tears that run
The desires that are hidden in secret
And dreams that are lost and gone.

Sometimes I seem so far
But that's when I'm really near
And every time you ask me "WHY"
To your finite mind,
My answer can't be clear.

That's why I want you to trust this life,
Every bit of it,
In My hand.
Seek to hear My voice
And just wait to understand...

The Same Prayer Again

Lord, you are never tired
But, if I was you
I'd be...
Because it is always the same prayer
That you receive
From me.

Prayer for a purpose
And an instrument to be
To know my Master's dream
And fulfil it
Through all my deeds.

A daughter to you, Father
Beating Your heart in mine
Seeing beyond the obvious
And to learn what's in Your mind

But just know this Lord;
That I'll never say "No"
To anything you say;
Yes, I'll throw a tantrum
But in the end, I will obey.

A pen;
Or a broom,

Anything I can be;
As long as I'm working for
Your demands.
Living every moment
With joy and satisfaction
That I'm used by my Master's Hand.

Help Me Be a Miracle

You are the Lord of miracles
You healed the blind
When the banquet declined
You even provided wine

You raised the dead to life
You delivered the demoniac from strife
More than 5000, you fed at a time
You changed a Samaritan woman's life
Yes, you shifted paradigms.

The winds and the waves obeyed your voice.
When you said so,
The fish in the sea
Surrendered to the nets
They departed to their snare
They even unveiled Peter's heart
And brought him to his knees.

On the way to the cross
You restored Malchus' ears
Before you breathed your last
You sweat blood
Not tears

So many miracles

In three of years of life
But the greatest of all
Was when you paid the price
For all the filth in my life

You know my secrets
And my guilt within
Yet, Your love is too powerful
To stay away from my sin.

What you did on the Cross
Was not just history
Your Grace oh Lord
Changed my destiny

Lord, help me be a miracle
Every day, every time
Let me help someone see the sunshine
Or at least a silver line

Help me to heal
Help me to see
Help me to be the miracle
Somebody needs.

I Heard Them

I heard them in the dark
Someone whom I love
Saying things about me
That I could not believe

Disappointed me
Betrayed me
Hurt me
Let me down
Made me bitter
Turned my mind around
I never doubted their loyalty
But to them, I was an obscurity

Yes, it was an unguarded moment
Maybe it was a harmless comment
I don't think they meant that junk
Maybe it was their foolish tongue

Love is patient
Love is kind
What they said, I'll try to not mind.
I will forgo
I have been forgiven
So I will forgive

Praying because He's Risen

Early in the morning,
The women went to see where His body laid,
But the angel declared,
"He has risen, do not be afraid"

John went to the tomb, he didn't break a stride
In the tomb, Peter stepped inside

But the burial cloth folded,
'Twas all they could see,
Everything was kept tidy and neat.

Mary, whose life Jesus had changed,
Stood drowning in tears
Weeping because they took her Lord away.
She turned to hear someone say,
"Woman, why are you crying?"
She hoped this gardener would tell her
Where His body lay.

But "Mary", He called.
She knew this voice.
The voice of Her Master
The one who rescued her,
Her Lord of all.

Two friends walking towards the Emmaus
village
With their face downcast.
Discussing the sad climax of Christ
Another stranger,
With them, he joined,
And as He spoke, their hearts burned.

"Come with us", they offered him to stay
He went to their home, and it was almost late,
As the stranger took the bread,
Broke it and gave them to eat
They saw the stranger was Jesus Christ,
Who they thought was forced to die.

Later that day,
He went to meet
His trembling disciples,
Scared and weak.
Hiding behind doors,
Unable to face a future they could not see
"Peace be with you"
He stood among them and said
"With Flesh and bones
I have returned
Touch me and see,
Let's also have some fish to eat"

With the amazed disciples,

He sat to eat
He opened their minds,
The Scriptures, He revealed.

Then the disciples went along,
To a mountain in Galilee
Jesus was there,
To give them the authority
Over sickness and strife.
To give them the power,
That made Him come alive
"Make disciples of the nations,
Teach them to obey.
I am with you
Till the end of age"

Lord, this Easter
I only pray
That I see this power
Work on me every day.
Not in ways that others are deceived
But to help each one trust in You and believe.
For every man and woman,
To surrender to your love.
To be your true disciple
And glorify You with their whole lives.

Please, Lord.

Sorry Lord, I was Angry at the Kids

I'm grateful Lord for my children
I remember the anguish of my labour
Savouring my birthing victory
I also remember your favour

But today God
I was so mean to them
Grumpy, yelling, and berating
Impatient and debating

Forgive me, Lord
My unjust tirade
Help me to see
How helpless they are
The wonder in their eyes
Their life and laughter

My every moment with the children
Let me treasure
The disorder and chaos
Must become my pleasure

I am an untidy child myself
But still, you are so patient with me
You bear my messiness, my awkward life
You are kind, you offer me respite.

Help me to have your heart, oh God
These children of mine
Let me remember that they are loaned from the
Divine.
Let me treat them with patience and love.
Let me wait to see them shine.

The Walls

My walls are ever before you
My walls of self
My walls of despair
Sometimes my walls of words and pain
You can see through all of them
Yes, my walls of ego and blame

Jesus, you never stay behind the walls
Sometimes you knock
And to show yourself clearly
Sometimes you walk through them all

You rebuilt the walls of Jerusalem
But Jericho's walls - you destroyed
Rahab lived because of the rope over the wall
Didn't a basket by the wall save your servant
Paul?

Your gentleness breaks the walls in my heart
Your cords of kindness tear it down
Your ropes of love move the weight from my
shoulder
So many walls you turned around

Help them too Lord
Those hurting inside
The walls that they have built on their own
The walls that keep them prisoned inside

Where they cannot see any hope, any light
Break those walls, Lord
Let them be
Close to you Lord, happy and free.

I'm Sorry Lord

I'm sorry for the questions asked
I'm sorry for being rude
I'm sorry for being bitter inside
I'm sorry that I didn't depend on You.

I'm sorry for forgetting Your Love
Your ultimate Sacrifice
I'm sorry that I worried so much
Thinking that Your Grace won't suffice.

I'm sorry I thought that I'm all grown up
And became so mature in faith;
That I dared to push Your plans behind
And let my desires take its place.

I'm sorry for the grumbling
I'm sorry that I blamed
All the blessings in my life
To be the reason for my pain

Lord, please forgive me
And give me one more chance;
I'll remain in perfect peace.
Trusting You to meet more than
Just my daily needs.

Though I'm clumsy
It's because of Your Grace, I am called
To live for Your Glory
And to care for Your flock

Maybe not in ways
That I have dreamt it to be
But surely in Your mind
There is an assignment for me.

Angry at My Spouse

Ah! He ignored me again
He broke my heart
Without saying a thing
I know that words, they pierce like darts.
But did you know that silence stings?

Why do I love so much?
My heart is sore
My head hangs low.
Am I using him as an emotional crutch?

May the exits of my mind be open
Every word in my mind unspoken
A gentle answer can break a bone
But sometimes, you need a heart of stone

Repetitive fights
They never end
Neither of us
Can ever bend
Oh how we preserve our ego
Missing every opportunity to forget and let go.

We brought between us
A foggy pond
Filled with distress and clutter

Shrouded in mysteries, we cannot see beyond
A million miles away from each other

Everything is blur
And what we speak
We cannot concur

But we wait for that magical moment
When this too shall pass
When our feelings surrender and
And our love outlasts

But Give Me Jesus

When the perils are many
The profits are few
Yet, they say
Punish me if you may, but give me Jesus

Problems make them dizzy
Doubts make faith fuzzy
Though their path is not easy.
They say,
Mock me if you may, but give me Jesus.

They have known loneliness
Alone in the light
Watching the city in darkness
Misunderstood and rejected
Yet, they say
Leave me if you may, but give me Jesus

Friends and family they leave behind
Will never renounce their faith
Now or any other time
Even if they are looked at suspiciously
And made to pay a price instantly,
Yet, they say
Kill me if you may, but I will live for Jesus

The Church

We have different stories.
We walk our own journey of faith.

Some of us are strong,
Some of us are weak,
Some have hope,
And some never rise to see dawn

Some overcome sin,
But some are tired of failing.
Some rejoice
And some are mourning

Don't judge and fret
Because He's not done yet.
God is writing a beautiful story
Through each of these lives,
Touching, shaping, and transforming to glory

The church is a place
Where you can come as you are
The church is a place where
You can ask questions from your heart
The church is a place where
Feelings are heard
The church is a place

Where your shame is covered
The church is the place where you can learn and
know
A disciple of Christ, you become
And grow.

When I Don't Know What to Pray

It is crazy how my mind seems like a clean slate
But there's still so much to say
But oh! How the words
They wither away.

All the answers I need are with You
But I struggle because I don't know what to ask
I want to fall into your arms and cry out loud.
But, I don't know where to start.

That's why I offer a prayer to say thanks
For all the things that You have done
For knowing me and loving me
For being the only One.

I'm thankful for the things I never knew to ask,
but You were thoughtful to provide.
I'm thankful for the things I asked every day,
but You, in your wisdom, chose to delay.

And I'm thankful that Your grace
Let me be Your child
And yet another moment,
Let me stay...

My Thangachi

"A baby sister is born"

Was what that aunt said
I scratched my head
Wondering,
Shouldn't it have been a brother instead?
Because that's what everyone was saying
And asked me to pray
And I believed so much
That it was a brother on the way.

But who cares, I just needed a sibling
Someone with whom I can play
Someone to take to school with me
And someone who listens to what I say.

Thank you so much....

For being my best friend
For bearing all my torture
For all the endless errands you've run
For being the only encouraging one
And knowing me as I want to be
For calling me Akka
A title I'm so proud to receive.

I thank God so much
For your wisdom, beyond your years
I'm glad that you've become a woman of
substance
And learnt so well to handle your fears.

Many books you bought me
Beautiful and bright
Hoping that, there is much I will write
This time,
You did not hope or wait
You pushed me through
And I wrote this book.

Thank you, Annie.
I love you.

Ambitions

Oh, how much I admired doctors
A surgeon I wanted to be
Mending organs
Saving lives
Important and in authority

But I did not score so well you know
To deserve a seat as a medico
I put it away, my desire, my dream
My love for physiology remains supreme

I remain in peace because I know
That I belong to a bigger plan
That I am not alone
And every step is in His hand

And now, I try to be many things
Teaching a class
Writing a book
Being a preacher perhaps
Oh! Hearken me the family cook

Your fingers are clumsy, said my art teacher
Maybe my hands were never meant to hold a
scalpel
Hurting hearts, and confused souls

Wearied travellers, I gently grapple

I want to be that beautiful woman
With a willing heart and busy hands
The futility of my days, I do not bemoan
I hold the bible in one hand, and a pen in the
other
A soup for the sick, a song for another.

When Parents Age

There were days when I was a child
I wished my parents played by my side
They ran busy lives
Brought to us what the home required

But lazy afternoons
Cuddled up together
Listening to stories and eating ice-creams
Long walks on the beach and playing in the park
Was my idea of happiness

Now, in the stage between adolescence and
death
That we call adulthood
I'm caught up
Pursuing my own dreams and passion
Doing things that I call ambition

And I see my parents age
I suddenly don't have time
To listen to their stories
When they talk about their aches and pain
It feels like a bore
I don't want to hear them again

These people who are the secret to my being

Whose blood gave me substance
Whose genes gave me my essence
Even if they are weak today
I have seen their many strong and plenty days

I hope I never become
Too busy for them
Let my love and gratefulness
Lead the path and beacon
To be patient and kind
As my parents age on.

Adoration

I love you, Jesus
So much so that
I'm filled with awe
Every day every hour

Sometimes I ignore you
But I can never deny you
Every sinew, every cell,
Your mercies they tell

The paths so far
The lessons so dear
Experiences learned in joy and fear
You always showed up
You were always there

A wretched wreck my life would have been
Confused priorities
Mistaken identities
Futile qualities
Despicable moralities

And I still fail you
So many times
But the Lord of the universe
You reach to be mine

What you have done to my soul
Is deep and healing
You've changed my views
My peace unfailing
Thank you for your amazing grace
Every doubt is gone
When I see your face.

I love you, Jesus.